UNADORNED
IN LOVE,
IN BED,
OR
BEDDING

UNADORNED IN LOVE, IN BED, OR BEDDING

Wisdom Confucius Could Have Shared But Didn't

Yang Hanlun

PARTRIDGE

Library of Congress Control Number: 2019931699
ISBN: Softcover   978-1-5437-4854-3
                   eBook   978-1-5437-4853-6

Print information available on the last page.

To order additional copies of this book, contact
Toll Free 800 101 2657 (Singapore)
Toll Free 1 800 81 7340 (Malaysia)
orders.singapore@partridgepublishing.com

www.partridgepublishing.com/singapore

For Fiona, Allen, and Ian.
In memory of Grandma.

But true wisdom comes from those very wise who also are human.

—An old saying

By Way of an Introduction

A few centuries ago, or more I think, when this now modern world was, as they say, old, meaning not as modern as it is now—ancients came up with, if you think about it, quite a straightforward tenet. It's one that everyone I know, even in the very small circle I move in, seems to know—an exhortation, if you will. And it's very simple for anyone and everyone—which is most—to follow.

In plain English, nothing being plainer (except, nothing surprises us; ancients were already ahead of their time, dabbling in exponential mathematics), it translates as follows:

Go forth and have a thousand sons and ten thousand grandsons.

With the ancients' kind permission, I'll stay true to the ever relevant and true *yin yang* principle to change, only just slightly, this tenet for our modern times. But wait, you say. Shouldn't it be 2000 + 20,000, not 1000 + 10,000? No, I'll leave it at that. You know what I mean:

*Go forth and have 1000 sons and daughters +
10,000 grandsons and granddaughters.*

Now, a few centuries, or less I think, after that,
the land whence the ancients (those abovementioned)
came became the most populated on earth. So the
tenet/exhortation actually works! That's very (meaning
but too) well. To this day. And this as ancients, wise and
prescient as they always were, foresaw.

But, of course, we, like everyone else, had already
seen it coming.

Yes, as we shall see, we had *it* coming.

What we didn't see coming, and were too afraid
to ask, was this: Why *not* this modern world of ours?

Truth is everyone seems to know there's no need
for exhortation in this age we live in. Not us moderns,
thank you. You, I, and everyone else see it every day
and everywhere—every what, every whom, every
when, and every how. It's around, outside, us. At the
same time, it's within, unmistakably inside us, never
leaving us. It pervades, invades, and just radiates—all
across our modern society. Inescapable, inexorable,
and seductive. We fall for it, we can't live without it.
We ask for it. We don't ask for it. We get it. No, it's
not all subliminal at all. But it's quite sublime, if you
think of it, and we wish for and want it that way.

Yes, it is an exhortation in *spirit* where, in this now modern world, there's no need for such an exhortation. (Does it sound as if we're missing something here? Ah, yes, ancients, well-meaning as they might have been, underestimated us moderns, who've obviously come a long way.)

So, here it goes, what could not have been plainer than plain English, this *modern* exhortation that needs not an exhortation:

Go forth, being surrounded, and live by sex, and just continue having it, and even more of it—never mind the 1000 + 10,000, etc. (Copy, the venerable ancients, with our sincerest apologies.)

Now that that's stated, as clear as a cloudless noonday, and since nobody—I mean nobody—needs the tenet/exhortation, it's none of anyone's business, least of all mine, anymore. No longer do we need to linger or say more here.

Let me, therefore, quickly summarize this *paradoxical* situation that, as moderns, we're in:

It's an exhortation—in fact, *not in* spirit—*in which and where there's not a real need for in this modern world in which and where there's a real need for it.*

There, encapsulated! Just as ancients would and usually did. Simply stated (not that I, no, not an ancient, am being asked): What happened to us? It's a crying shame, if you ask me. In our progressive, next-computer, next-phone world. We lost and are losing by the day. A palpable loss, irrecoverably, to the future.

That's not good if you think about it, for isn't future what progress is about?

What can we, you and I, do? Like all of us, I've absolutely no clue. (I wouldn't just be writing if I had the answer, would I?)

Worse, the ancients are dead. Gone.

But seriously, if no one has seen this by now, this has become quite tendentious. I'm just doing my bit. In this not-so-brave new world that we live in.

That is, I am earnestly doing so here, even, yes, even if no one absolutely has a need for this, or for that matter any, exhortation. Ancient, or wise, or both, it may be.

What is the book about? In an inspired moment under the hardly fruiting, old, and gnarled mango tree (I happen to live in the hot, humid tropics, like Grandma), I described it to myself as a book on the 'philosophy of sex (or love)', or the 'philosophy of the sexes (or love)'. (The choice was deliberately between a non-fruiting tree, like that which inspired a great religious thinker, or a fruiting one, like that which inspired a scientific giant—but, in indecision, I just picked the old faithful mango.) But *Philosophy*? Of *Sex* (or *Love*)?

P and S (or L) look like they're getting into an argument, even at the outset.

P: I'm Philosophy—uppercase P.
S: No biggie (ha! ha! caught you there). I'm SEX—
sans *lowercase.*
P (mockingly): Oh, I see. You've learnt French. In the course of work?
S (street-smartly): Perhaps you too can learn it. From me. Visit me sometime?
P (seriously): No, thanks. I've better things to do.
S (coyly, eyeing him, nudging, tugging at his sleeve): Who better to do than with me?
Do you want to? Not going to ask again!
P (emphatically): No!
S (baiting): You're too dry!
P (quite seriously): No, you're too wet!

So the argument goes on …

I decided, since it's obviously getting nowhere, that *P* of *S (or L)* is out.

And then, at this point, I remembered the ancients. It's in moments like this that I take a leaf from their book:

A picture is worth more than a thousand words. (I now seriously think that it's hyperbole, not exponential, mathematics, but when ancients say it, it doesn't really matter, does it?)

So, yes, to clear any and all doubts, the book is a picture. Or one that comes like a picture. Little bits in it that make up a picture. Like inked brushstrokes of leaves of bamboo trees in a paper-and-silk painting that, in sum, 'form' a picture.

One, the little bits, or brushstrokes, that point to something along the lines of a *P* of *S (or L).* (You see, some do not give up too easily, do they?)

The trick is to look for it, the little bits of quivering strokes of an author's (like a painter's) brush.

Or, alternatively, if you choose not to see it (the picture) that way, you can read the book as a *love story*, with the little bits that it would consist of. But it is one, unlike modern love stories, with no characters in it. No heroes or heroines for to find.

No, I am not being disingenuous. Or devious. As far as I'm concerned, one first must buy the book, then read it. That's how it works.

Choice of the main title of the book. Now *that* could be the picture, at least a clue to it. As the ancients (who else?) said ever so long ago, a saying that still rings (but not in my partially-deaf ears) unerringly true today:

Same bed but different dreams.

In other words, the one who one now has, who's warm (or is it hot?), nicely cuddling snugly in one's bed (or, "Norwegian Wood"-ish, not one's bed), should be the one who one loves, or is married to, and therefore absolutely desires.

Whichever is the case, that's how things work, or should work. However, sometimes—let's just say—the one who one has is *not* the one who one is presently supposed to love, or to be unmarried to, or to absolutely desire. That is, the ancients were spot on. (Not, oh no, that it's their fault.)

So, I wanted in the title of the book, for the sake of everyone, every kind of situation and all bets covered, and that it be inclusive of the likes of many.

That's just the way things are and always will be. No fault of yours. Or mine.

Choice of the book's subtitle. Among the ancients, the rock star of the time was none other than Confucius. There is a story about him (he being that popular) that I was told when I was younger. (Actually, that's how it all started for me.) The truth to the story, however, cannot be verified, not by me, it being that long ago.

Confucius, it is said, had a propensity, in his great wisdom, to put women (and, of course, to be fair to him, men) in their rightful place. He divided women into two groups: whores and mothers.

As the story goes, one cloudy noonday in those otherwise crummy ancient times of yore, he was asked *that* one question, in a rather timorous, and hence respectful, tone by someone in the audience—who's therefore not a rock star. As it turned out, that unknown one in the great crowd (for it was always very crowded when Confucius was in town) who remains to this day, unlike the sage himself, unknown, had the temerity of being unable to help himself but ask the question. It seems he was—even in Confucius' disarming presence on that dusty day—somehow mindful in his common, very simple, and therefore unwise mind of some whiff, even if just a little, of partiality. Hence, probably being personally aware that even among the whores in all of whoredom there are those (even if just one) who are as highly worthy of true motherhood as any mother he or any like he could name, he softly, and especially respectfully—but pertinently—asked, "Sage, where do you put *your* dear mother?"

By all accounts, Confucius was stumped. Yes, caught, once only, off guard. Very not Confucius. Unlike him. But, like any rock star we know, he soon regained his composure, which was not very long after, and moved on.

Mentioning a rock star in the subtitle of a book, even if ancient (or dead), is not too difficult a decision not to give a miss.

How I came to write the book. No, it's not *Kama Sutra*, which is also of yore, some books of which are venerable and others not despite being of yore. The fact is there are books written which are not sex (or sexy) books *per se* (by these, I mean the *Fanny Hill* kind) but books of sex jokes that oftentimes begin as follows:

Someone walks into an English (or is it *Scottish* or *Irish*?) *bar, and ...*

So, I thought, why not write a book along the lines of some neo-ancient sayings, tenets or wisdom, on love and sex, or the sexes. On the subject of love, marriage, or passion, in the bedroom or out of it. (Writing in the form of sayings I'm only taking a leaf from the book of ancients!)

Yes, somewhat contrarily, or perhaps ironically, this is a sexy but serious book on love and sex, or the sexes. (I thought it might just work.)

Of course, on the subject of writing, I *do* like the writings and plays of George Bernard Shaw. (Another name that pops to mind is Voltaire. Or Oscar Wilde. And Groucho Marx. Or even Bob Hope. I do like *all* of them. But, I think, one is enough here.) Well, GBS and I both write in English, for me as first a language as my native (actually grandmother) tongue. The difference, of course, is he's English, writing in English, and I'm not.

By the way, since we're on the subject of writing, when ancients made paper, as only they could, ancient they might have been, and later, printing, and printed books of stories and novels, those bestsellers of yore (yes, even in those somewhat crummy times long ago), some of these had no punctuation. Quite James Joycean, don't you think? No, don't worry. I won't do this here.

Ah, yes. I forgot to mention at the outset: I *do* come from a long line of ancients, many of them living from the time of none other than Confucius himself, those very wise ones, with their great hand-me-downs, some of which I really do hope rub off on me, in *spirit* at least, if nothing else. And in this way, remember the ancients, and their true wisdom. Something that I, too, tend to forget. No longer; I will never ever forget that paper and printing are not the only benefaction from them.

But that was long ago, a very long time ago. Way before Grandma left her birthplace, which, by the way, is in the aforementioned land of the ancients. As she told it, she had no tear in her eye. It was heart-rendering and tearing. Then, when all was not hopeful, no, not at all, she left her birthplace—that's neither hot nor humid like here but had very cold winter months, being in the north, almost near the Great Wall—in the great upheavals of the 30s, which nobody asked for. Many years later, on a windless, hot, and humid afternoon, when she had a firstborn grandchild she chose to name, she said, ever mindful of the old stone-and-wood home she left, never to see again, "It was the best trade-off to the great Great Wall."

For me today, I'm just this—*glad*—that she left, and survived the wars, rampage, torture, killings, annihilation, rapes, pillage, destruction, and uprooting of a great many people—and later to be Grandma, just Grandma, with her warm silk-and-linen lap.

What could have been was, very fortunately, *not*.

Grandma. Without any anger. Rocking the past in the lull of the tropical glow of the warm evening sunset, a repository to me, from childhood, of everything she was, had lived for and in, and had known—a living link to the past of great ancients. Her past, that did survive—across great seas, far from her birthplace—the wars, rampage, torture, killings, etc. Without it, and if not for those undyingly wise ancients who lived before and from the time of Confucius, this book might not have been written, seen the blindingly bright light of a tropical noonday, and printed. And by that, I don't mean this here ubiquitous piece of whitish and acid-free paper I'm now holding in my hands (although we could be writing on papyri or, worse, reading off the wall, think of it) or the printing press.

***

So here you have them, the wise sayings Confucius could have told, in his time, to us moderns but, as it turned out, didn't.

And for this impatient, next-update, modern time of ours, you could almost hear them, like rustling bamboo leaves, coming from his ancient lips, quivering ever not-so-slightly, not too unlike him, who has no longer been around for so long now.

But don't *quote* him. You probably already know all that he has said and means.

It's the fitting homage I can only pay to him—to whom you and I (or at least I) owe a great debt and the greatest of respect. You know, I do owe him one, or maybe two.

I've tried countless times to organize and arrange them, like the leaves (not a ripened fruit on my head) falling from a still bending but never-breaking old bamboo tree, those very many leaves, in some form, to put them in some semblance of order. I even thought of placing them under headers, or categories, say, the *good*, the *bad*, and the *ugly*. But then, I thought, by the time anyone reaches the *ugly*, it would have made for very depressing reading indeed. Not too good. Better to leave the unpredictable, the disorder. This way, even if I didn't make your day, at least I didn't spoil it for you to regret, after the event, buying the book.

In the end, therefore, my plan to arrange, or re-arrange, them was to no avail. I decided totally against it (not that I didn't try). This very disorder, and any inaccuracies in them, are therefore, mine and mine alone. Neither the venerable sage's nor anyone else's.

A final point, with my sincerest apologies to the ancients. (How many times must I say that?) I have, throughout the book, taken the liberty of updating the language to one a modern reader will easily understand, so as not to miss the point even, or especially, of ancient wisdom. As everyone knows, this can happen (lost in translation and all).

***

There you are—Confucius' could-be tenets or wisdom for our no-longer-ancient, advanced, and very busy age. This is where you, having barely started, now must go.

Take your pick, *what*, *where*, *when*, *how*, and to *whom* you want to read them, these ink-printed brushstrokes of rustling bamboo leaves, and then go—just *go*.

Unadorned in Love, in Bed, or Bedding

Wisdom Confucius Could Have Shared but Didn't

Love comes with or in many forms and norms, phases and faces, sighs and thighs, lips and hips, sorrows and 'morrows, dimples and pimples, cries and dries, joy and coy, moans and groans, sin and din, eyes and ayes, legs and aches, hope and nope, lies and tries, sad and cad, heaven and craven, "hey" and hay, leaves and heaves, laid and 'fraid, bosoms and threesomes, silence and violence, chasing and facing, fools and tools, nos and gos, seeking and peeking, "hi"s and highs, honey and money, kisses and misses, begging and nagging, take it and leave it, only and lonely, marrying and parrying, ranting and panting, skirts and flirts, sobbing and fobbing, meeting and cheating, hugging and tugging, moons and swoons, biding and fighting, tears and fears, pecking and necking, hiding and sliding, tying and untying, railing and failing, pain and gain, teasing and pleasing, blushes and gushes ... and so it goes, on and on.

Love's the only waking dream we live in to wake to.

Love is forever; it outlives us.

Lies matter to love as truth, for
without these, it is not.

Those who do seek out those who don't, and
those who don't seek out those who do as
those who do seek out those who do, and those
who don't do seek out those who don't.

If we live only for the one we love, we live
with the consequences without it.

It's not should as could in love.

Love: who gets who, how, why, where, and when.

To be fair is asking what the other can't give.

Love's often no farther than the next
available seat on the train.

Giving all of oneself can bring little return or none.

Toss and turn in bed in love as
toss and turn without it.

Falling in love is as we trip.

Love breaks all rules, even those it itself just made.

Absence makes the sex work harder.

Unmistakable the sighs in love
as the sighs without it.

If love moves mountains, mountains
are quite hard to move.

If love's a toss-up, there is only
one of two outcomes.

Love's a glow that's not missed or too far
away but next to you for you to find.

Trouble in love won't go away
for one, not the other.

Never underestimate the power
of love to underestimate.

Hope's the flame that keeps love
alive, but mind the flicker.

To live with it in love is to live without it.

Love honestly attracts dishonesty
just as it does honesty.

Nothing stops desire being love as love desire.

To die for love would end it all.

If it's a catch, beware the snare.

Little things never little are in love;
great things are little without it.

Love not taken seriously might be there;
taken seriously, it might not be there.

The only closure that love seeks is itself.

To be in love is to miss the train and still board it
in the next station, the next, and yet the next.

Sharing's never love's but what's all for itself.

You won't believe it happens until it happens.

Love is only itself to account for without it.

Opportunity is no different for
love as for sex to take.

Love holds no promises that cannot be fulfilled
and no promises that can be fulfilled.

If there's a key to love, there's a lock.

Innocence finds in another's
innocence all it hopes of itself.

Forgive oneself nothing that another would not.

To give in and then think not, think and then
give in; that's easier than you think.

Breaking up is hard to do; falling was easy.

To hate in love is a paradox.

Nothing compares with you is still a comparison.

Same dream but different beds.[1]

Remember, love is also only a word.

Love's not a habit till it's one.

Doubt little another's sensibilities as doubt one's.

Laugh not at love lest it's you.

---

[1]   With my apologies to the ancients.

Gently, gently tread in love if gently
not, gently not, tread without it.

Absence makes the heart grow fonder
in being missed to know otherwise.

Marry for money is an alliteration;
might not just be too.

The fire of sex and passion does
flicker; goes out too.

Always try not too easily to give in to love
or sex unless want to, and then give in.

Love for love's and sex for sex's
sake are just repetitive.

Innocence attracts too the not innocent.

Thinking of it never is or will ever be good enough.

Pull wool over the eyes, but try
pulling away the sheet too.

With love, its own laughter cures its heartaches.

Goodnights, as adults, are not only for the children.

Love yet the will not that cannot be, as
sex the must not that will not be.

Candidly, it's candid as to sex as honest as to love.

Love wears a face all will recognize.

A loveless love is an oxymoron;
that's not to deny it.

Available assets bank on sex.

Sex, we are no fools for it, yet it
still fools of us makes.

If a situation's too complicated, try
avoiding it in the first place.

When committing it, admission could never
a virtue be any more than it requires it.

Love requires very little but of you.

Unfaithfulness hurts, but
dishonesty hurts absolutely.

Who dares wins may still lose.

Love may forgive everything but not you.

You can always still prove love wrong.

When sex is for the asking, don't.

Repenting changes little the fact.

Seduction is almost always halfway there.

A new love is only relative to an old.

Till the end of time is too far
away when we are dead.

Infidelity always provides another alternative.

Youth experiences what experience no longer has.

A scandal is only scandalous when
it becomes a scandal.

What one often can't offer, another can.

Harder to confess than to be discovered,
which makes it harder.

Love's a mystery only two would go
through the trouble finding.

Adultery commits it when discovered.

Catch me if you can, that'll land not
just you, but me, a catch.

Love is both judge and jury.

There's no jade skin that may not later be
regarded as no longer jade by the jaded.

It's not that there's no love in sex
as there's sex without it.

As with all else, love does tire sometimes.

If too much sex is bad, think too
much sex that's good.

Only fools fall in love; for us, who're no fools,
this cannot be true; so none has fallen in love.

Love is only sweet as there's bitter.

Sex is only as addictive as one.

Love shows the way, but we could still be lost in it.

If love is blind, just see what those who can't.

It's not what skirt or trouser hides but who dons it.

Always follow your heart to what follows on too.

Adultery is love or sex by other means.

Nothing is whispered in love that's not whispered
before; sighed that's not sighed before.

Frigidity is not willing.

To be sorry could be truth, or a lie.

The happy and ending are a paradox.

Sex lusts forever.

Lying in love could be told while lying down.

Two's a crowd; three's company.

Till death do us part is the end.

There are highs and there are lows,
but neither's the worry.

Nothing that's apparent in love that
is not apparent without it.

Unfortunately, not to love is to take sides.

Betrayal hurts and hurts absolutely in love.

Love at first sight at least is a start.

Sex gratifies, and it gratifies one—or better, two.

To love is to go down the very same path
none has gone but has gone before.

Two to tango, three to tangle.

Ideal love, if there were, has the not ideal.

And they leave happily after.

"Why?" just asks too much than "Why not?" in sex.

Harder to take back words than give them.

Love, receive it; sex, accept it.

One's reputation precedes one for one to have it.

Love's different for all and no different
for beggar and king or queen.

Turning back the clock presumes the present.

Marriage on the rocks brings on a bad hangover.

Marrying up or down is relative to one.

If there's something to hide, try not
to bring it to the bedroom.

When found out, denying is one option.

More of the same in sex and passion too.

Age love forgives that age does not.

Not to have sex, yet wanting it, rapes the mind.

Nagging is only relative to the one listening.

Wars fought over a woman or man
cannot be blamed on her or him.

Not to be tempted by temptation is not
not lacking in wisdom but lacking in it.

To be unfulfilled is love's foil.

Hindsight was blind then, not now.

Platonic love requires none.

Make your own bed and then dream in it.

Forgive the fault if aware of the knowledge of it.

Reason's love if reason's needed, but
reason's love if reason's not needed.

Locked out of the house could sometimes
be better than locked in it.

There's more to sex than just sex. More sex.

If it's not going anywhere, try going home.

It's not that being in love requires little of
lies as that it requires none of you.

Eyes have it as thighs have, but lower.

Titillation works to titillate too.

Temptation is not if you're tempted
but if you're still not tempted.

Love might not be wasted on the young.

Pick on the one you pick makes no sense.

Did you or didn't you has never been
too difficult a question to answer.

Obscenity is only in the eyes of the beholder.

Never will I love like this again forecloses it.

The end of seduction justifies its means.

Who has not lost has not loved.

Grass greener on the other side is grass.

The chase presupposes a catch.

Unrequited love doesn't want it.

Kisses seal love more than words.

Better to have found to have lost it than
not to have found not to have lost it, but
better to have found not to have lost it.

A marriage is made in heaven when dead.

Cloud nine till it rains.

Being shy is by no means no
that's by no means yes.

Love may be lost, but tears do dry.

If prostitution is the oldest profession,
seduction doesn't need one.

In love neither beggar nor begged be.

Pass you by, all it takes, passed you by.

Better it is to leave the door slightly
ajar than fully open it.

Revenge that rights the wrong
wrongs to right no wrong.

Not just misery but sex loves company.

Sex may be improper but not love.

Nothing inconveniences in adultery
as another's knowledge of it.

As much love in ego as ego in love.

If it's any consolation, consolation only consoles.

Deny not youth its inexperience as
experience its experience.

What's behind closed doors stays behind closed
doors but who's going in and who coming out.

Same as before is either dull or not.

What's trouble doesn't often trouble till it troubles.

Meet expectations is expecting it.

Sex sells, but love buys.

Love proposes; one disposes.

Opposites attract justifies it.

Loneliness is not without love but because of it.

Two is a prime number divisible
by one or, worse, by itself.

Shame only comes in the way of
sex till sex overcomes it.

Love, as all journeys, begins with the first step.

Differently but not indifferently
in woman and man.

Sex, going by all that it asks, is suggestive;
it just can't not be suggestive.

Look before you leap and you won't fall in love.

One thing leads to another does happen.

If I had known better makes no one better.

Sex minds its and another's business as well.

If an excuse is needed try temptation.

Vows are just as good as who
makes them to whom.

Adultery presumes another love or none of it.

Flattery works not because it's not
honest but because it is.

Love suffers no fools but who's in it.

It's not that love does not make the saddest
music as makes the sweetest songs.

In love, we cross another's path to never again cross
another's path that cross another's path we may.

Love's unlikeliest and likeliest outcomes
always redound to you.

A moment of weakness except a moment
of weakness excuses all in sex.

A go to requires a come on but does not.

Lipstick stains sheets more than tears do.

To take for granted is quicker
than we could grant it.

Pour out all your heart in love
but mind it spilling over.

If a love or marriage seeks a purpose,
it's to make it purposeful.

Do not do unto the other that you would
not have the other do unto you, even if the
other may not not do unto you that he/she
would not have you do unto him/her.

Beauty is only in the eyes of the beholder
prefers none who will prove it.

Frivolity in love can never be frivolous.

Perversion is never an aversion to sex.

Those who live in glass houses
have but to wear clothes.

Sex, passion, and love too have much
in common in matters of time.

It's not as if sex was invented only yesterday,
but it lasted all night last night and day too.

It's not war, but capture another's
heart or surrender to another.

It's not true novelty that's no longer
cannot be found elsewhere.

"Come hither!" whispered one to the
other, to which "Go thither!" replied
the other, coming hither.

It never will only be when it comes
to if you will only let me.

Not who wears it, but the blood red, or
if you prefer, the deep blue, stocking
attracts too who wears it.

You're my everything leaves absolutely
nothing to you and, with you, who with you.

Oh! To wish to fall in love and stay in it
or to fall in love again and stay in it!

Not only with love but to be loving
you always could bore.

One-night stands do not want to be denied it
but do want to commit it without committing.

One's a pig; the other, a bitch. Can't they get
the damn animal right and it be the same too?

Naughty, naughty! but has reference neither to
very young children nor to grown grown-ups.

If it's Fate, or in the stars, you did not, cannot, do
not, and never will matter to whom who's very
dear to you, who did not, cannot, do not, and
never will matter to you very dear to who who's.

What, in the end, is love but to two in it?

Jealousy is what you have or could lose another
cannot have or could gain, and who must not and
will never ever be allowed to, as long as you live;
or what another has or could lose you cannot have
or could gain, and who must not and will never
ever be allowed to, as long as the other lives.

But seek and you will find will find you not
who all you need not seek you will find.

What's pure and what's profane cannot but the
same be in the first letter you spelt them with.

And yet how many times has it to be
told sex practised this way may be
detrimental to one's health?

Modesty just wants and desires; but says,
what I really want I am not going to say, and
what I really desire I am not going to say; and
what I really want and desire that you want
and desire of me — I am not going to say.

Love said *ad nauseum* to make the world
go round everyone knows, in the laws
of physics, doesn't. Ditto sex.

Sex not be rushed; 'tis done when 'tis done.

Life's not fair; love with it.

If you must not, try not to talk in your
dream when you sleep, if you must.

Refuse, or then to have to refute.

All's fair in love that's unfair without it.

Memory remembers all that's to be remembered
and all that's not to be remembered that'll be.

Faint hearts do not win fair ladies; heart feints do.

Spoiler alert! Someone knocks on the door.

Romance lives the life that a life
less lived that cannot can.

Sex without love may be nasty, brutish, and short.

Take a chance on me has a way out of it all
if only you will take a chance on me.

Love and passion till married.

Not that history does not repeat itself
as that it learns not and does.

Death and taxes and a life without love.

Now what is now wished for history
and time do not change.

In sex it's not who would but who wouldn't.

Who is no longer with whom may
not as cold be to hold.

If sure, do; unsure, trust your instincts.

Ask no favours to give none but do.

Can't you see it? is an unnecessary question.

Not wicked but who wishes what of whom.

Sincere asks sincerity of the
insincere and no more of it.

Laugh not at another's sex.

Tact is not doing what another won't but you do.

Less talk, more do, please.

If it's not below the belt, what is?

Virtue is a reputation and a loss at
the same time till no more.

Money never ensures love but does.

All philosophical or spiritual could only
come in the way of the physical.

A bird in hand could be worth more
than two, or three, in the bush.

Boredom encourages.

Sugar-coating is coated to the extent
needed to coat it; the less, the more.

No fruit falls without shaking.

A face and a body to die for will only kill you.

Dating soon becomes dated.

Beauty till goes to the head.

Whatever it be called, sex, neither
good nor evil, is sex.

One who may lie to another, yet another,
and to the world, to oneself cannot.

Being cheap is so undervalued.

If it's faults and defects, it's invariably
denying one's faults and defects.

What is left of love is never for keeps.

Once desired, then wanted no more,
not a desired state, once was.

Lies as a means is always justified by their ends.

Marriage, not a matter of chance, and what
comes of it, precisely is made out to be.

Perfect and defect have more letters in
common than you're prepared to find.

What could not be more inappropriate for the
occasion when appropriate for it than sex?

The situation one finds oneself in is always
predicated on one, and no one else.

Is it the fury that's no fury like the fury of
one scorned, or is it just not getting what
another can't give that another must?

Marriage works. Try it.

Brains and brawn or beauty are
not exclusive but are.

Love never differentiates who's
refined and who's not.

Some like it hot; none like it not.

Careful. Sharp tongues cut one's mouth.

Passion and sex are not only in
the head but much lower.

Love owes you a lot more than you can repay.

None looks over the wall unless prepared to find.

Regrets only are after the event.

Deeply in love presumes shallows.

Affairs never are fair.

Vanity is just more than one is.

Never take it at face value to face it.

A sore loser is never just upset for having
lost but sore because another has won.

Coy pretends innocence.

Sex does not one the younger make,
but it never ages one, does it?

But visit it and you may never want to leave.

No hard feelings, but the worst sex
is one that comes and goes.

There's no denying it: sex is not
just for babies but is.

If looks kill, don't.

Constancy isn't always in love
but none else to have it.

You don't need a celibate be to
know what marriage isn't.

Sex. It's everywhere. So why is it so bad?

Spite does much more than love can.

Question is: how do you know if it's fake
or pretend if it's fake or pretend?

It's a case of if you're not with
me, you're with another.

Or you pretend.

Can't buy love, but what would I not
give to spend a night with you.

The last time I checked, you were with me.

The quick brown fox jumps over
the lazy dog. Married life?

It's undeniable, the quiver of lips
or the quivering thighs.

Everything's forgivable, even yourself.

Contrary to perception, appearances do count.

It's being toward. Work on it.

It never is subtle if you don't want it to be.

The heartless just have less and not more.

You can't imagine just how often the
loaded question is asked time and
time again: Do you love me?

Undressing's the least of problems,
but do leave a few buttons on.

Riddle me this. If words cannot describe just
how, how then to hold them to their word?

It's common-place, your or my.

What's there that was not there before
already makes it a miracle.

Despite itself, shyness is its attraction.

Love, too, can be very naughty. Ditto marriage.

Explaining can't be helped makes it worse.

Vulnerable, or worse, at the mercy of.

Love needs not corroborate.

Desire more or less is how satisfied are you?

In seduction, pride comes after the fall.

For what it's worth and lacking make it
up for what it's worth not lacking.

Committing it is always to fill a void.

Unhappiness is only relative to whom.

If impossible, climb the window,
but possible the stairs.

Pleasure must be seized all at once, or it'll soon
be over only too quickly but must not be seized
all at once or it'll soon be over only too quickly.

The greater the hurt the greater the need to
get to the bottom of it to undo it (the hurt).

Avoiding the issue is always a way out of it.

As one door of hope closes, you can
always try opening another.

Sex is to no good therefore to seek for.

Not but in love as in marriage.

Sex, desire, or passion has no use of
philosophy, as it has none of them.

Nothing concerns sex more than itself as
nothing concerns it less than itself.

To be married always seems good beforehand.

Nothing is preposterous, particularly sex.

Nothing concerns marriage less than itself
as no more concerns it more than itself.

Love's that same worn park bench
in fall whom to still sit with.

What do you find in another that you cannot find in
me may be a paradoxical question but may not be.

Come what may in no way
predetermines it in any way.

The inexorable paradox of domination:
weakness none else it can overcome.

Beauty is only skin deep, but—Oh!—
those porcelain-white thighs!

Adultery is between even if not
among consenting adults.

All by myself is by no one.

Sex seeks none no less than the vulnerable.

Tease is yet to please just for now.

Nothing's too sheer or folly, not the thinnest tunic.

Marriage is what's left of a lover or two.

Respectability needs it, it cannot be without
it; even, and especially, when it is without it.

"Let me go!" pleads the one heart that's captured.

Being nice isn't love but being very nice.

It's only inadvertent that
indiscretions are not discreet.

It's either cheat or steal; in love, a heart.

The continuing paradox of a romantic
love story or a fairy tale: but only a
romantic love story or a fairy tale.

The key to wedlock is to keep it always in wedlock.

There's so little we can substitute honesty
with except with so much lies.

Demure is never ever too shy being too shy.

Tongues loosen as thighs, or looser.

Turn your back once, maybe
twice; that's all it takes.

Always expect the unexpected, better
or worse, love, sex, or passion.

All you need is loved for all unloved.

Free sex is as it's not sex free.

Adultery outside marriage is still love.

Love, unlike wine, doesn't need to be
aged; like wine, it ages well too.

Trust is not doing what others
do which you will too.

The power of love: without it, we're powerless.

What imagination is not limited
by you can't imagine.

Nothing, even the probability of love, is impossible.

At arm's length or hold in your
arms is a short distance.

All suspicions are either suspicious or not but both.

No greater fall is there than fall in love.

Sex whets the appetite, then doesn't.

Feeling another's pain isn't as painful.

Adultery fits a gap in marriage.

All that's forbidden is not forbidden
after but only before.

Sex one can do without but not two.

Never, even if only for a moment, think
that love is sex by another name.

Clothes beauty wears not to cover
but to hide only that to be seen.

Contrary to every hope of revenge, what goes
around does not always come around.

There can be, to love, no two ways about it but one.

Nothing compares with first love as there is none.

Lessons in love are learnt in it while not.

Who's lovesick not a disease has but no cure.

You're one in a million leaves little chance it's you.

One pants; the other rants.

In jealousy, uncovering the truth
is not an end but a means.

No beauty like the beauty of love hoary
and old or shrivelled and wrinkled.

Sex but not love gets straight to the point.

Love hides its face not because it's hidden or
it's secret but for you only always to find.

That too good to be true needs be true to be true.

Sex and desire if you must; love if you can.

Guilty pleasures only take from them.

Choose from: infidelity in marriage with no
love or fidelity in marriage with no love.

Desires dissipate in the heat of passion.

Fobbing needs that to fob off.

In sex means and end come happily together.

Found in bed together says more
than a thousand words.[2]

Fetishes are not another but of another.

Is it Cupid or cupidity?

Harder once with the mask off after putting it on.

Once smitten, twice shy it is not.

Lover's pet or lover's spat?

Flirting keeps you always in mind.

Jealousy doesn't erase it that never wants to.

Harder to appease once it
happens when it happens.

Even if one has one's wish, what one does not
wish to wish away when in love one cannot
but now wish to wish it away without it.

Unlucky in love or the worst hand?

---

[2]   With my apologies again to the ancients.

Whichever point of view you take
in marriage, there are two.

Sweet nothings are but cannot only
be the exchange of nothings.

Take your pick—half-empty or half-
full, i.e., half-lies or half-truths.

"Don't you even think about it" means that you
should stop thinking about it; which you are.

Flattery is how you wish it be said never
needing to have to say it yourself.

Indulgence seeks your indulgence to indulge in it.

Love is that near beyond that's within your reach.

In sex, you too can take a different position—by
that, we do not mean missionary or otherwise.

Sex and spiritual is not an alliteration;
marriage and spiritual is.

Masochism pains at pains to make it a pleasure.

Guilty makes sex a pleasure that makes it a sin.

If you must blame it not on moonlight.

Sex's once, or twice, removed from marriage.

Marriage when you don't doubt it.

Cruelty in love or marriage rides roughshod over it.

Narcissism is just all you want that you have.

Sex, hate it or love it. Ditto marriage.

The physical never ever comes in the
way of the philosophical or spiritual.

Morality lays down what you can't do
that others approve but you don't.

Love expectancy today—mean measure of time
anyone stays in it, or is expected to stay in it, today.

Sex's no cloak-and-dagger but cloak-and-without.

Many hands do light work make
under the silk tunic.

As you doubt sex overcomes it.

Marriage: only love's two-way mirror.

Sin and sex never should an alliteration
be (for marriage and sin, just to take an
example, will thus an alliteration be).

Love's the only waking dream
we live in we wake to.

Note on Translations

Go forth and have a thousand sons and ten thousand grandsons—千子万孙qiān zǐ wàn sūn

A picture is worth more than a thousand words—一图胜千言 yī tú sheng qiān yán

Same bed but different dreams—同床异梦tóng chuáng yì mèng

Yin yang—阴阳 yīn yáng

Printed in the United States
By Bookmasters